Treasury of Illustrated Classics™

Little Women

GIANT COLORING BOOK

©2004, 2005 Modern Publishing, a division of Unisystems, Inc.
™Treasury of Illustrated Classics is a trademark of Modern Publishing, a division of Unisystems, Inc.

®Honey Bear Books is a trademark owned by Honey Bear Productions, Inc., and is registered in the U.S. Patent and Trademark Office. No part of this book may be reproduced or copied in any form without written permission from the publisher. All Rights Reserved.

Modern Publishing
A Division of Unisystems, Inc.
New York, New York 10022

Printed in the U.S.A.
Series UPC: 49180

The March sisters were waiting for their mother to come home. Meg was the oldest. She loved to knit. Jo was the second oldest. She loved to read.

Beth was very shy. She loved to play the piano. Amy, the youngest, was fond of drawing.

Mr. March was away. He had been called for duty in the Civil War. His daughters missed him.

The family did not have much money. They knew
that there was no money for Christmas gifts this year.

The girls wanted to buy their mother presents with the little money that they had saved.

A Letter from Father

On Christmas morning, Jo found a gift under her pillow. Everyone had a gift!

Mrs. March was touched by her daughters'
thoughtful presents.

Mrs. March told her daughters about a poor family
that could not afford a holiday meal. "Let's give them
our Christmas breakfast!" the girls said together.

When they returned, they found a Christmas feast on the table!

Their neighbor, Mr. Laurence, had heard about their
gift to the poor family and sent the Marches a feast
to reward them. Mr. Laurence and his grandson,
Laurie, lived next door.

Meg and Jo were invited to a New Year's Eve ball.
Beth and Amy were too young to go.

"I wish I had a fancy silk dress to wear," Meg said. "Our plain cotton dresses will be just fine," Jo replied. Jo hated to dress up!

Jo's dress had a hole in the back. Meg told her that she must stand with her back to the wall at the party so that no one would notice.

At the party, Meg joined a group of girls. Jo stood against a wall. She did not care for gossip.

Jo stood alone for a while. Then she slipped behind
a curtain into another part of the room. She was
surprised to see Mr. Laurence's grandson there!

"Pardon me," Jo stammered. "I didn't know anyone was in here, Mr. Laurence."
"Please call me Laurie," the young man said.

In the ballroom, Jo and Laurie danced together.

Jo noticed Meg waving to her from across the room. Jo went to her sister. Meg was pale. She rubbed her ankle.

"I twisted my ankle," Meg said. "How am I going to walk home?"

"I'll take care of that," Laurie said, as he scooped up Meg.
"I will take you home in my grandfather's carriage."

The next day, Jo went to visit Laurie.

She hoped that they would become good friends.

Jo and Laurie talked for hours. "Beth says that I never know when to stop talking!" Jo laughed.

"Is Beth the quiet one who stays home a lot?"
Laurie asked. "And Meg is the oldest one. Amy
is the youngest one. Everyone seems so cheerful
at your home."

Laurie showed Jo his grandfather's library. There were so many books! "What riches!" Jo exclaimed.

As Jo looked at the books, she heard a voice behind her. She turned as Mr. Laurence entered the room.

"Laurie seemed to need some company," Jo said nervously. "I was just trying to be neighborly." She thought that Mr. Laurence was a stern man.

"It's quite all right, Miss March," Mr. Laurence said
politely. "Let's have some tea."
Before Jo left, Mr. Laurence asked her to visit again.
He told her to bring her sisters along, too.

As time went on, the March sisters began to feel at home in the Laurence mansion. Jo loved the library. Amy copied pictures to her heart's content.

But Beth was very shy. She was afraid to go with her sisters.

Mr. Laurence thought of a way to get Beth to visit. He asked Mrs. March, "Would one of your girls like to play my piano? I need someone to keep it in tune."

Beth enjoyed playing the piano more than anything else. She agreed to go.

A few days later, Beth went to the Laurence mansion.
She played the piano for hours.

To thank Mr. Laurence, Beth sent him a note and
made him a pair of slippers.

A few days later, Beth returned from an errand. Her mother and sisters were excited. When she walked into the parlor, she saw a brand new piano waiting for her!

It was from Mr. Laurence!

One Saturday afternoon, Amy saw Meg and Jo getting ready to go out. "Where are you going?" Amy asked.

"We are going with Laurie to the theater," Jo said.
"You cannot come, " Jo added quickly.
Amy was furious. "You'll pay for this, Jo March,"
Amy cried.

Meg and Jo had a wonderful time at the theater.
But Jo felt bad about Amy. When they got home,
they found Amy sitting in the parlor.

Jo wondered what her little sister could have done
to get back at her.

When she went to her room, Jo noticed that her journal was missing. The journal contained many years' worth of Jo's writing!

Jo stormed downstairs and demanded that Amy give
her back the journal.
"I threw it into the fire!" Amy yelled.
"You wicked girl!" Jo cried. "I will never forgive you!"

Later that day, Amy saw how miserable Jo looked.
Amy felt bad about burning Jo's journal.
"Please forgive me, Jo" Amy pleaded, but Jo refused.

Then one day, as Jo was leaving to go ice-skating with Laurie, Amy came downstairs.
"Oh, please forgive me. I want to go with you," Amy cried. Jo ignored her and walked out of the house.

Amy followed Jo and Laurie to the frozen river.

All of a sudden, Jo and Laurie heard a cry from the middle of the river. Amy had fallen through the ice!

Jo was too scared to move. Laurie pulled Amy from the freezing water. He saved her life!

"It would have been my fault if Amy had died," Jo said to her mother. "My temper got the best of me."

"It was an accident, Jo," Mrs. March replied. "But never let your temper run away with you again!" Jo hugged her sister warmly.

When Spring arrived the March sisters spent their days gardening and walking through the fields and meadows.

Laurie thought it would be fun to set up a post office between his home and the March family's. Then everyone could leave messages for each other.

Since Beth liked to stay at home, she was elected postmistress. She liked the job of distributing the mail.

One day, Jo received a letter from Laurie inviting her and her sisters on a picnic. Laurie's tutor, Mr. Brooke, would also be there.

The next morning, the girls were very excited as
they dressed for the picnic.

The party set off in two boats.

When they arrived at Longmeadow, they ate their picnic lunch.

After lunch, they played games. Meg and Mr. Brooke sat off to the side. They enjoyed a lovely conversation.

When fall came, Jo spent most of her time in the
attic, writing stories.

One day, Jo told Laurie that she had left two of her stories with the local newspaper. He said he hoped that the newspaper would print them.

Laurie had a secret of his own. "Mr. Brooke is in love with Meg," he reported. Jo was upset.

A few weeks later, Jo ran into the parlor, waving a newspaper. "One of my stories has been published!" she announced.

Her family was very proud of her!

Not long after that, a telegram arrived for Mrs. March. Mr. March was ill. Mrs. March had to go to him at once. Mr. Brooke was to accompany Mrs. March.

Before they left, Jo handed her mother a large sum
of money.
"Jo, where did you get all of this money?" Mrs.
March asked, surprised.

Jo removed her bonnet. She had cut off her hair and sold it!

Beth went every day to visit a poor family that her mother had cared for. The children were very ill. Beth caught the fever, too.

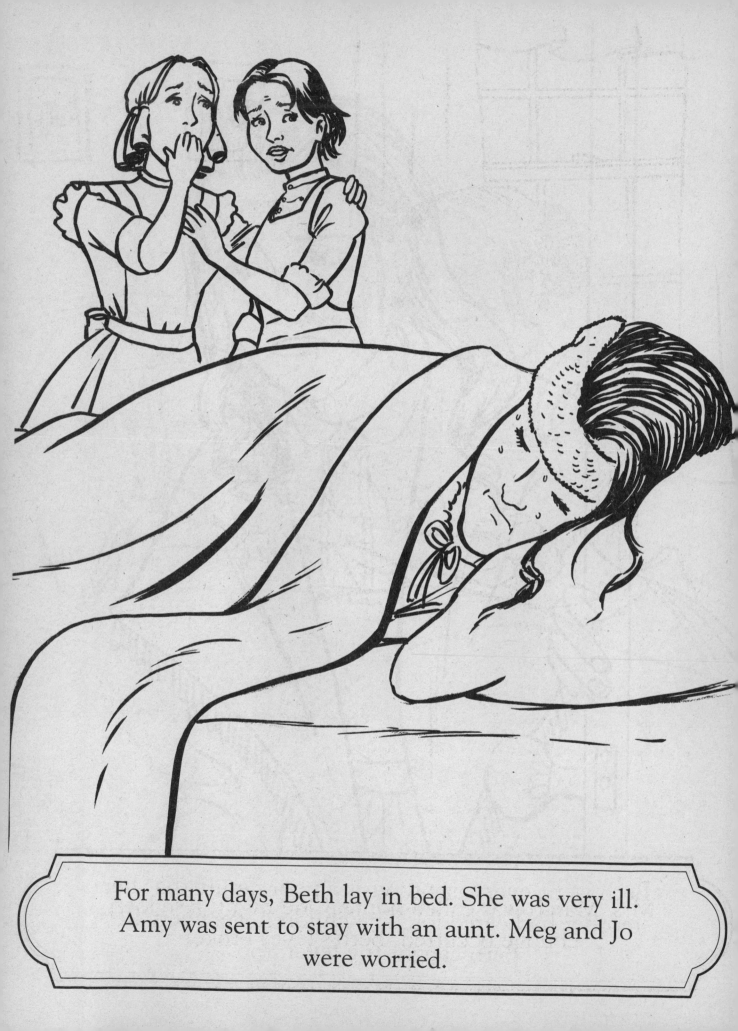

For many days, Beth lay in bed. She was very ill. Amy was sent to stay with an aunt. Meg and Jo were worried.

Mrs. March was called home. One night, a sudden change occurred. Beth's fever broke!

On Christmas morning, Laurie gave presents to Mrs. March and the girls. Then he looked into the parlor and said, "Here is one final present!" It was Mr. March, home from the war!

The girls were overjoyed to have their father home
with them for the holidays.

For the next few years, Mr. Brooke saved money so that he could marry Meg.

On a beautiful June day, Meg March and John
Brooke were married.

Late the next summer, Jo and Laurie visited John and Meg, who were celebrating the birth of twins. Jo held the girl, named Daisy.

Laurie held the boy, named John, Jr.

One day, Amy was invited to go to Europe with one of their aunts. Jo was jealous.

But everyone else was sad to see Amy go.

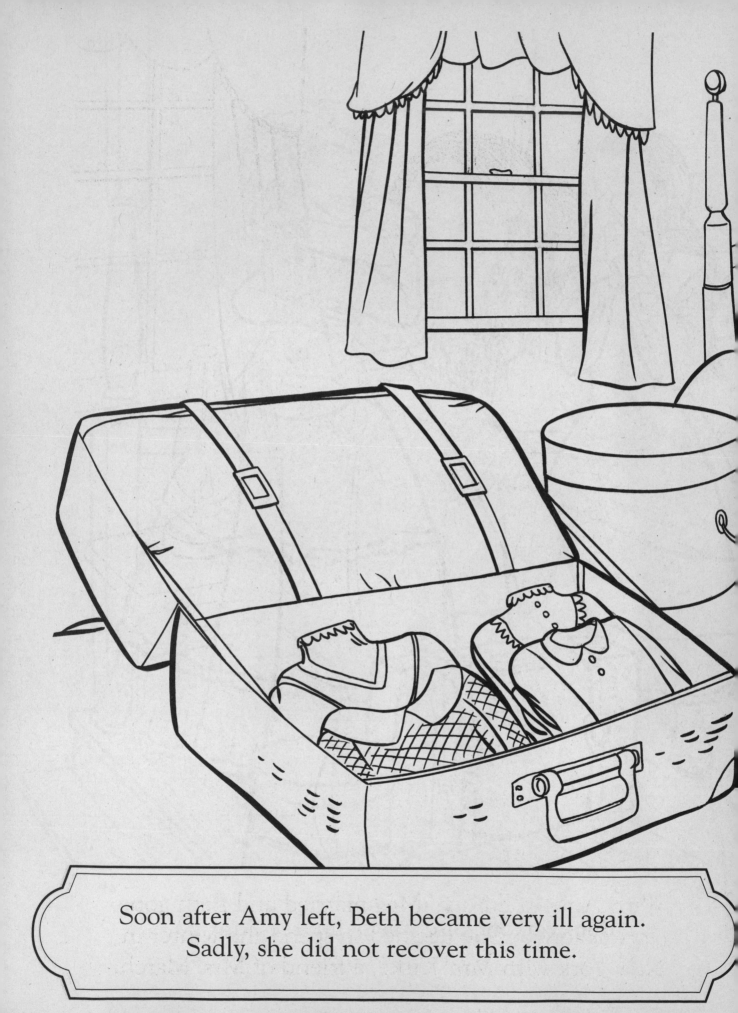

Soon after Amy left, Beth became very ill again.
Sadly, she did not recover this time.

With Amy in Europe, Meg married and Beth gone, Jo was lonely. She decided to spend the winter in New York with Mrs. Kirke, a friend of Mrs. March.

While Jo was at Mrs. Kirke's boarding house, she taught Mrs. Kirke's children to read and write. Mrs. Kirke's other boarder, Mr. Bhaer, was a professor.

Mr. Bhaer and Jo spent a lot of time together. Soon they were good friends.

In June, Jo returned home. She was sad to leave
Mr. Bhaer.

Laurie told Jo that he loved her. Jo did not want to hurt Laurie, but she said that they must remain friends only. Laurie was angry. He decided to go to Europe with his grandfather.

Laurie thought that he would be angry with Jo forever. But in a few months, he was able to forgive her. He discovered that he loved her as a friend, as well.

In Europe, Laurie spent a lot of time with Amy. They fell in love and were married. Jo was happy when she heard the news.

In the attic, Jo found some old notebooks and a book that Mr. Bhaer had given her. She missed him more than ever.

When Amy and Laurie returned from Europe, the
family celebrated their marriage.

One day soon after that, there was a knock at the door. When Jo opened the door, she saw Mr. Bhaer!

On her way into town the next afternoon, rain
began to fall. Out of nowhere, an umbrella appeared
over Jo's head. Mr. Bhaer was holding it.

"Jo, I want to marry you," Mr. Bhaer declared. "I came
back one last time to see if you felt the same way."
"I want to marry you, too!" Jo cried.

Jo and Mr. Bhaer were married. They had two sons and opened a school in town.

The Marches and their new family and friends spent many happy times together. They knew that there was no greater joy than being together!